# STEPPING OUT
## a Lent resource

PETE TOWNSEND

Kevin Mayhew

First published in 2001 by
KEVIN MAYHEW LTD
Buxhall, Stowmarket, Suffolk, IP14 3BW
Email: info@kevinmayhewltd.com



The material in this book first appeared in *Café Logos,* Years B and C.



9 8 7 6 5 4 3 2 1 0

ISBN 1 84003 831 4
Catalogue No. 1500467

Cover design by Angela Selfe
Edited and typeset by Elisabeth Bates
Illustrations by David Bill

Printed and bound in Great Britain

# Contents

# Acknowledgements

Since my first faltering steps on the road to adulthood, I've bumped into, trodden on, laughed with and shared many an embarrassing moment with far too many people to mention. Some faces are now distant memories while others are constant sources of amusement.

Above all, I must thank Ruth for having the strength of character to laugh off my frequent attempts at being grown-up. To Dale, Nathan, Esme and Laurie, I suppose you're stuck with a dad who doesn't understand the meaning of the word 'sensible'. And to Liz I offer a grateful smile as she consistantly deals with my written offerings as if she knows what she's doing . . . impressive!

To all my other friends on this journey . . . thanks.

# Introduction

*Stepping Out* is all about the journey to the cross and a few steps beyond. The period leading up to the crucifixion was a time when Jesus firmly established who he was, what he was all about and why he was here.

*Stepping Out* takes you on a journey. It's a little bit more than simply deciding to go somewhere, jumping in the car and, before you've turned the first corner, asking: 'Are we there yet?' This is a journey that takes in all the bits between the start and the finish.

*Stepping Out* starts with the baptism of Jesus and the beginning of his journey to the cross. We follow his verbal duel with the devil, we watch as he slowly reveals just who he is, we get to know him a little more as he spends some time with friends. After a display of anger at the Temple, we're perplexed about his talk of an early death, we stand in awe at his entry into Jerusalem and then stand bowed as his talk of death becomes a reality and, finally, we rejoice at his resurrection. In the end, we realise that the journey has only just begun as Peter steps in to remind us about God's love for everyone.

*Stepping Out* is a journey of reflection, amazement and wonder. It's a time to examine God's love as revealed in his Son. It's also a time to recognise that just as Jesus 'stepped out' and gave his life for each one of us, we should also consider *Stepping Out* of our comfort zone and accept the challenge to demonstrate God's love to the world.

Each unit is divided into six sections with icons for easy recognition:

**Planning the journey:**

An introduction to the Bible reading and main theme.

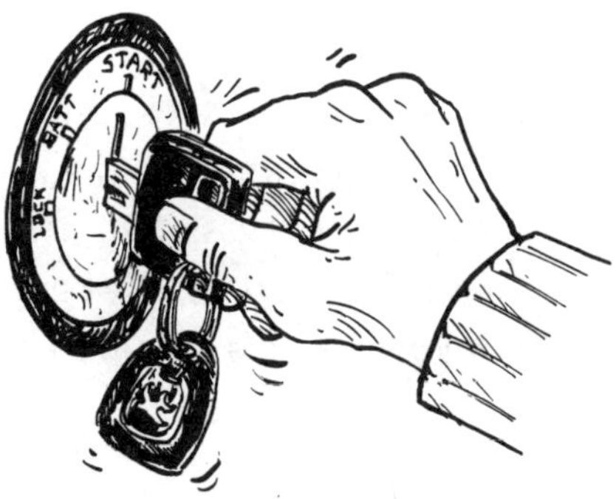

**Starting out:**

An idea for activities which may help focus the group on the theme.

**On the road:**

An introduction and link to the teaching, using some ideas for worship songs.

**Driving:**

The main teaching bit with further ideas and guidelines for sharing.

**Clocking up the miles:**

Some more ideas for discussion and thought.

**Further on up the road:**

Some suggestions for reflection and prayer.

The references to worship songs are only suggestions. You can substitute other material on a similar theme if you prefer. You can either use the worship songs as part of group worship or use the lyrics in discussion. All of the worship suggestions can be found in *The source*, *The source 2*, *The source new songs*, *Re:source 2000* and *World Wide Worship No. 1,* all of which are published by Kevin Mayhew Ltd.

# Getting wet

## Mark 1:9-15: The baptism of Jesus

**Equipment:**
large plastic bowl filled with warm water
bar of soap
plastic bag filled with wet mud (or you could use cocoa powder mixed to a paste)
music and lyrics

Display the bowl of water on a table at the front of the room. Put your hands into the bag containing mud/cocoa and enthusiastically cover your hands in the mixture. Tell the group that someone told you that covering your hands with this mixture would improve the look of the skin. Once you have covered your hands (keeping the mixture on your hands) go to one of the group and ask them to shake your hand and tell you if your hand feels softer! Ask why they won't touch your hand.

Ask the group if any of them would like the mixture put on their face. Now wash the mixture off! Will anyone shake your hand now?

Ask the group what the problem was with having 'dirty' hands. Why did they feel uncomfortable about touching the mixture? Why did washing your hands make a difference?

**(Allow 10 minutes for this activity)**

Have a look at 'For all that you've done' by Dennis Jernigan (*The source*, 108) or 'Great is he who's the King of kings' (*The source* 2, 705).

You might like to use a similar piece of music which reflects the same theme. Have a copy of the lyrics available.

**(Allow approximately 5 minutes)**

What did the group think the lyrics had to say? Did they make any sense?

**Read Mark 1:9-15**
Jesus was around 30 years old at the time of his visit to John the Baptist. Jesus had waited for the right moment to begin what he had been sent to do.

- Firstly, Jesus recognised that the time was right, that the moment had come for him to make that decision to leave the comfort of Nazareth and start his ministry.

- Secondly, Jesus wanted to identify with the message of John the Baptist. John was reluctant to baptise Jesus, knowing that Jesus was without sin. But it was important for Jesus to identify with the need for forgiveness of sin. It was also a symbolic act. Jesus was to take on the sins of the world (see John 1:29) which would lead to his death on the cross.
- Thirdly, as soon as Jesus came out of the water, the Holy Spirit came down like a dove. The Holy Spirit was to guide and encourage Jesus for the journey ahead.
- Finally, a voice from heaven said, 'You are my own son.' This was a recognition of Jesus and what he had decided to do. It was a fatherly nod to say, 'Yes, you are mine and I'm really happy with you.' This wasn't a 'pat on the head'. Both God and Jesus knew the way ahead was going to be far from easy but at least Jesus knew that he wouldn't be alone, he had his Father's blessing.

The baptism of Jesus was a 'decision' to go the way that God wanted him to go; it was submitting to his Father, accepting the Holy Spirit as encourager and guide for the way ahead and by following this step Jesus was given his Father's blessing.

Baptism is a way of deciding to start a new journey, of turning away from the actions that separate us from God, receiving God's blessing on our lives and having the Holy Spirit as our encourager.

The mud/mixture that was used in the 'Starting out' section is a way of showing how our past actions (sin) separate us from God. By washing (baptism) we have decided to turn our backs on the actions which got us 'muddy' in the first place and to start all over again (see Romans 6:3-11).

Place the bowl of water on the table in front of the group. Invite anyone who would like to come and wash their hands in the water. This is a symbolic way of turning our backs on any actions which we feel put 'distance' between ourselves and God.

While some of the group wash their hands (don't expect all of the group to want to take part in this) read the following prayer:

Father God,
this water is great
when we're thirsty, we're hot, we're dirty,
and when we're showing you
that we don't want to hang on to anything
which keeps us away from you.

Not our actions or our inactivity
    nor by giving in to thoughts that suggest
    we look away from you and your love for us.
We wash our hands
    as a symbol of our decision to follow you;
    as a symbol of love for your ways;
    as a symbol of thanks for your Son. Amen.

## Luke 4:1-13: Jesus and the devil

**Equipment:**
paper and pens
candle
music and lyrics

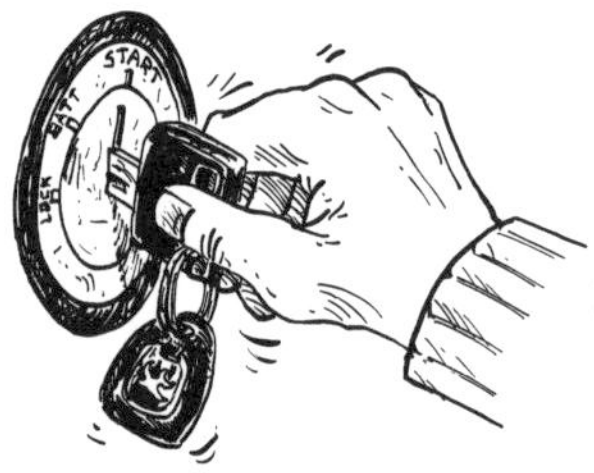

Give each member of the group a piece of paper and a pen, and ask them to write three statements about their hopes or desires on the piece of paper (don't write any name or initials which might identify the writer). For example:

1. I want to build a boat.
2. I want to become an actor/actress.
3. I want to travel around the world.

When each group member has finished, collect the statements, shuffle them and then distribute them around the group. Ask one group member to read the three statements and see if the rest of the group can guess who wrote the statements. To add a little bit of mystery, have some statements already prepared which are not specific to anyone in the group. These statements could be based on someone you, or the group, knows or be entirely fictitious. Some of these statements could be totally bizarre!

**(Allow 10 minutes for this activity)**

How well do we know each other? How well do we know ourselves, particularly when we are faced with a really difficult situation?

Take a look at 'He is the Lord' by Kevin Prosch (*The source*, 159), or 'Is it true today?' by Martin Smith (*The source*, 241).

**(Allow approximately 5 minutes for this)**

It isn't always easy to be confident or certain about what we know or believe. It's especially difficult to be positive and self-assured when we are in an awkward situation.

**Read Luke 4:1-13**

Jesus had just been baptised in the River Jordan and a voice from heaven had said: 'You are my own dear Son, and I am pleased with you' (Luke 3:22), when he goes off into the desert for a few days. This was to be a period of preparation for Jesus and he was possibly looking forward to some time on his own before things started to heat up. No sooner had he put a foot in the sand when the devil starts to have a go at him. Possibly Jesus sighed and thought: 'Well, there goes my peace and quiet!' Having just been acknowledged as God's Son and told that his Father was pleased with him, along comes someone to question everything.

The devil started by saying 'If . . .'. It's a question, a seed of doubt, a prod at Jesus' self-assurance. By then Jesus was hot, tired, hungry and thirsty. It certainly wasn't the best time to start fielding difficult questions. Jesus could quite easily have replied, 'Right now isn't a good time to answer questions' or 'Let me sleep on it', but he knew that he'd have to face these challenges sooner or later. His answers were part reply and part reassurance to himself. He needed to respond to the devil with words that not only refuted the devil's 'if', but also reaffirmed what Jesus knew to be true.

It's important to remember that the words Jesus used in his replies were not just some simple quotes that he recalled from his childhood, but were true statements, an underlining of his knowledge of who he was and what he had to do.

It's never very easy to feel confident when we are in a difficult situation and someone asks awkward questions. You know that when a question starts with either: 'I thought that . . .' or 'Are you sure that . . .' it's going to be tough finding the appropriate answer. There are many situations where it's tough for us to feel confident in what we believe and 'if' we are doing the right thing. Ask the group if they can think of any situations which have made them question what they believe or doubt that they are doing the 'right' thing.

Make a list of some of the following statements and see if any relate to the situations discussed:

- I am God's child. (John 1:12)
- I am Christ's friend. (John 15:15)
- I have been bought with a price. I belong to God. (1 Corinthians 6:19-20)
- I am complete in Christ. (Colossians 2:10)
- I have been forgiven. (Colossians 1:14)
- I am born of God and the evil one cannot touch me. (1 John 5:1, 18)
- I have direct access to God through the Holy Spirit. (Ephesians 2:18)
- I have not been given a spirit of fear, but of power, love and a sound mind. (2 Timothy 1:7)
- I may approach God with boldness and confidence. (Ephesians 3:12)
- I am confident that the good work that God has begun in me will be perfected. (Philippians 1:6)
- I cannot be separated from the love of God. (Romans 8:39)

There are many more Bible verses which you might add to the list.

**(Allow 5 minutes)**

Ask the group to reflect on the Bible verses that you have discussed. Light a candle and while the group are quiet, read the following:

Psalm 138:7-8.
I am surrounded by trouble,
    but you protect me against my angry enemies.
With your powerful arm you keep me safe.
You, Lord, will always treat me with kindness.
Your love never fails.
You have made us what we are.
Don't give up on us now!

# Going down a storm!

## Luke 8:22-25: A storm

flipchart
table-tennis balls
bowl of water
marker pens
music and lyrics

Write a list of phobias from the selection below. Don't write the meaning of the phobia, that's for the group to try and guess.

| | |
|---|---|
| Monophobia | (fear of loneliness) |
| Nyctophobia | (fear of night) |
| Zelophobia | (fear of jealousy) |
| Ergophobia | (fear of work) |
| Algophobia | (fear of pain) |
| Scopophobia | (fear of being looked at) |
| Ochlophobia | (fear of crowds) |
| Thanatophobia | (fear of death) |
| Kakorraphiaphobia | (fear of failure) |
| Odontophobia | (fear of teeth) |

The group might have a lot of fun just trying to pronounce some of these words!

Reveal one phobia name at a time and see if the group can guess what the phobia is a fear of. You might like to have a go at inventing some of your own phobias, e.g. footaphobia (fear of football), brussophobia (fear of brussels sprouts) or even soapophobia (fear of soap operas).

**(Allow 10 minutes for this activity)**

Being afraid shouldn't be something to fear! It's how we deal with fear that is important. Take a look at 'Hold me closer to you' by Noel and Tricia Richards (*The source*, 172) or 'You are my rock' by Jarrod Cooper and Sharon Pearce (*The source*, 597).

**(Allow approximately 5 minutes for this)**

Have a brief chat with the group about fear. What is fear? Why do we get afraid? What kind of things make us afraid?

**Read Luke 8:22-25**

It seemed like a good idea at the time. What could be better than sailing on the lake and having a bit of relaxation?

Jesus had suggested sailing across to the other side of Lake Galilee to an area populated by non-Jews. With him, amongst the disciples, were Peter, James and John, experienced sailors who knew the lake well. It was only natural that Jesus felt confident in the ability of the three disciples and allowed himself to catch up on some much needed rest.

Without warning, a storm appeared and threatened to sink the boat. This couldn't have been a run-of-the-mill storm. Peter and the others would have experienced many storms and lived to tell the tale. This storm must have been something out of the ordinary to frighten the sailors. Even with all their knowledge and skills they became so afraid that they turned to the only person they thought could help.

They didn't turn to Jesus because he was an amazing sailor or had any astounding skills when it came to weather forecasting. The disciples turned to Jesus because they had seen him perform miracles which defied logic.

The Bible verses simply tell us that Jesus got up and ordered the storm to stop making a nuisance of itself. From storm to calm within seconds and, having had his sleep ruined, Jesus merely asked the disciples why they didn't have any faith! They'd seen what he could do before, why couldn't they trust him to deal with this situation? Perhaps the disciples thought that if he was asleep he wasn't aware of the danger they were all in? Possibly, because all the other miracles had occurred on dry land, they didn't know if he understood the true threat of the lake?

Jesus calmed the storm and reassured the disciples that they were safe in his hands. A lesson for us all?

If we take the word 'storm' to mean any situation that causes unrest, discomfort or holds a threat, can the group think of 'storms' in their lives that are giving them cause for concern?

Do any of the group want to talk about the situation? Have any other members of the group experienced something similar? If so, how did they deal with it?

If it's appropriate, give each member of the group one of the table-tennis balls and a marker pen. Suggest that they write their name on the ball and place it in the bowl of water.

**(Allow 5 minutes)**

While the group think about the 'storm(s)' which affect their lives, read the following prayer:

Lord,
I realise it sounds daft,
possibly really stupid
in the warm light of the day,
but I just can't help
looking behind me
whenever I walk upstairs to bed.
Now, please don't laugh,
I know it's irrational,
that there's nothing there,
but you never know,
one day there just might be
something which will throw my life
into confusion, disarray,
and make it seem like
the sun's gone to sleep.

You see,
the stairs
are my life.
It's my journey
from birth to the future.
And I really need to know
that you're there,
right behind me,
beside me, in front of me,
watching my feet
so that I don't trip over my own shadow.

## Luke 9:28-36, 37-43: The true glory of Jesus

**Equipment:**
postcards
pens and paper
large envelope
music and lyrics

Write each of the following phrases on a separate card:

1. I feel like a . . .
2. My mouth feels like a . . .
3. After eating, my stomach feels like a . . .
4. Every time I watch TV my head feels like a . . .
5. After I brush my teeth, they feel like a . . .
6. When I sneeze, my nose feels like a . . .

Now, on some of the other cards write:

1. hole in the road.
2. packet of cornflakes.
3. bottle of disinfectant.
4. bag of sawdust.
5. compost bin.
6. bucket of cold custard.

Shuffle the first set of cards and ask a member of the group to select one of the cards. To complete the sentence ask another group member to select a card from the second set of cards (make sure that these cards are face down). Now, read the complete sentence. Replace the used card from the second set of cards and shuffle. Repeat the selection process with other group members. The whole game should raise a laugh or three. You might like to write some of your own sentences and make the second set of cards as wacky as you can.

**(Allow 10 minutes for this activity)**

Sometimes it's easier to express our feelings by actions. Some people have attempted to explain how they feel by putting words and music together in a way that reflects an emotion far better than words alone.

Take a look at 'You make my heart feel glad' by Patricia Morgan and Sue

Rinaldi (*The source*, 603) or 'I need you more' by Lindell Cooley and Bruce Haynes (*The source*, 226).

**(Allow approximately 5 minutes for this)**

Trying to express our emotions, especially to our family and friends, can leave us feeling angry, frustrated or vulnerable.

**Read Luke 9:28-43**

Jesus had been really busy. He'd spoken to literally thousands of people, healed the sick and dealt with a whole host of dodgy evil spirits and was now in need of recharging his batteries. Taking Peter, John and James with him, Jesus took a stroll up a mountain to spend some time talking with his heavenly Father.

As with many of us, as soon as their eyelids obeyed gravity, the three disciples were in the land of slumber. While they were creating a few snores, the disciples were unaware that something remarkable was happening to Jesus. Moses and Elijah had appeared and were talking to Jesus about all that was going to happen to him. Peter, James and John suddenly opened their eyes and were confronted by an amazing scene. The disciples must have looked at each other to check whether they were sharing the same dream! Immediately Peter began to talk about making the place special by building three shelters, or tents, to mark the place where something incredible happened. You can imagine what Jesus thought.

Before Peter could get on to the idea of building a hotel, shopping mall (selling replica models of Moses and Elijah) and amusement arcade, God's voice sounded from heaven, telling the three disciples to listen to what Jesus had to say. The three disciples were left speechless (perhaps a good thing, considering what Peter had been talking about).

The next day, Jesus and the disciples came down from the mountain and walked straight into a load of hassle. First, there was a large crowd waiting for Jesus to say something clever; second, a father worried about the demon attacking his son and third, complaints that some of the disciples had tried to deal with the demon but had failed miserably. Again, can you imagine how Jesus felt? Doh! Look at verse 41, as Jesus, in frustration, says to his disciples: 'Why do I have to put up with you?' Bit harsh perhaps, or is Jesus really annoyed that his disciples hadn't been listening to a word he'd said over the past few weeks?

Jesus dealt with the demon, and the boy and his father were amazed at God's authority and power. The interesting thing is that Jesus wasn't above feeling frustrated, annoyed or vulnerable. He wanted to trust his disciples but they were clearly found lacking in the listening and understanding stakes.

Jesus knows how we feel because he's been there already. Quite reassuring really.

Distribute pens and small pieces of paper to each member of the group. Ask the group to think about those areas of their lives where they may feel frustrated, annoyed, vulnerable, confused or hurt. Suggest that they write a single word which sums up the way they feel, e.g. ANGRY.

Ask them to place their piece of paper into a large envelope upon which you have written: 'For the attention of Jesus'. Place the envelope where the whole group can see it.

**(Allow 5 minutes)**

Ask the group to be quiet and think about the situation that is causing/has caused them to feel the way they do. Read the following prayer:

OK, Lord,
enough is enough.
I don't like feeling,
thinking, sensing, listening,
the way I do
to all those situations
which drive me up the wall,
through the ceiling and leave my head spinning.
You know how I feel.
You've been there, done that, read the book
and starred in the film.
Please be with me, help me, stand by me.

# This will hurt me more than it hurts you!

## Mark 8:31-38: Jesus speaks about his suffering and death

**Equipment:**
pen and paper for each member of the group
music and lyrics
small cross

Ask the group to close their eyes for a few moments. While they have their eyes closed describe the following scene. Suggest to the group that it would be good if they can visualise the scene as you speak.

> It's a really cold miserable day. Dark grey clouds cover the sky and a fine mist is swirling around. As you look ahead there is a large bridge across a deep river. A man is standing on the bridge, staring at the sky. Suddenly the man climbs onto the bridge railings. He is having trouble keeping his balance but this doesn't seem to bother him. He seems in danger of falling off the bridge and into the river far below.
>
> Running over to him, not wanting to frighten him in case he falls, you ask him if he needs any help. Before you can say any more he shouts at you to keep away, threatening to jump if you come any closer.

Now ask the group to write on their pieces of paper what they would say to persuade the man to climb down from the bridge to safety. Discuss some of the responses.
**(Allow 10 minutes for this activity)**

Sometimes it is difficult to appreciate what other people have done for us. Have a look at 'I know a place' by Randy and Terry Butler (*The source*, 209) or 'All my days' by Stuart Townend, (*The source new songs*, 2)
**(Allow approximately 5 minutes)**

Discuss the lyrics with the group. Were they able to appreciate what the lyrics were trying to say?

**Read Mark 8:31-38**

Jesus begins to tell the disciples about suffering, rejection and finally death. But it was only a temporary situation. Jesus explained that three days later he would be alive again.

The disciples had experienced some incredible times and seen Jesus doing amazing things. And then he ruins it by saying it's all coming to an end! What will happen after three days? What will happen to the disciples?

Peter was obviously not impressed. He took Jesus to one side and suggested it wasn't a good idea to talk like that in front of the other disciples. The reason that Jesus got so angry with Peter was that Jesus was being tempted to go in a different direction to the one he knew he should take. Jesus knew that he had to fulfil God's purpose and that a sacrificial death was the only way for humankind to be reconciled with God. Jesus didn't want to be 'talked out' of the way he was meant to take.

The disciples had seen Jesus do some awesome things but even they didn't know the full extent of what Jesus could do. As the Son of God, Jesus could have defeated anything the Romans or religious groups could throw at him.

Jesus was facing similar temptations to those he overcame in the desert. Did he really want to suffer? Did he really want to waste his life? Did he really want to disappoint all those people? Jesus knew that the only way ahead was for him to pay the ultimate price: his death on the cross.

Ask the group to look again at their responses to the man on the bridge.

What emotions would the group have felt about what the man was attempting to do?

- Was it a waste of life?
- Surely things couldn't be that bad?
- What about the people who cared for him?
- What about the future?

These were all emotions that Peter and the disciples would have felt. Were some of the group's responses similar to what Peter might have said? Can the group begin to understand how Peter would have felt and why he wanted Jesus to stop talking like that?

Although we should value life and not 'throw it away', Jesus knew that our eternal lives depended on him being the final sacrifice so that we could become part of God's family once and for all.

Place a small cross in the centre of the room. Suggest to the group that they might like to focus on the cross and think about how Jesus may have felt after Peter had spoken to him. Peter was speaking out of genuine concern for Jesus. Jesus knew this but didn't want to be tempted to ignore what God had asked him to do.

Think about the friendship Jesus had with the disciples and how the news of his suffering and death would hurt the disciples. This knowledge must have made Jesus feel sad. But there was no going back or altering course. The way forward for all of humankind was through the cross.

Allow the group time to reflect and consider. After a short time, close by reading the following:

Colossians 1:19-20.
God himself was pleased to live fully in his Son. And God was pleased for him to make peace by sacrificing his blood on the cross, so that all beings in heaven and on earth would be brought back to God. Amen.

# You what?

## Luke 13:1-9: Turn back to God

**Equipment:**
Lego or similar building blocks
wastepaper basket
pens and paper
music and lyrics

Divide the group into three or four teams. Give each team a box of building blocks and tell them that their task is to build a tower which will be strong enough to support a wastepaper basket (full or empty, it depends how tough you want to make the game). Before the game begins, choose one member from each team and ask them to behave as a saboteur in the building process. You might like to choose and brief the saboteurs before the session begins. The saboteurs are to make a nuisance of themselves by giving conflicting advice, knocking blocks over and causing as much hassle as they can. Advise the saboteurs that their behaviour should be planned carefully so as not to seem too obstructive, but enough to make it awkward for their team to complete the task.

After two minutes 'test' each construction with the wastepaper basket. It might help the saboteurs if you let the other team members in on the 'plot' to obstruct the building process.

Did any of the teams guess what the saboteurs were doing or did they genuinely think that the saboteurs were being a real 'pain'?

**(Allow 10 minutes for this activity)**

We are often shocked by people's actions and left wondering why they behave the way they do.

Have a look at 'Beauty for brokenness' by Graham Kendrick (*The source*, 37), or 'Have you heard the good news' by Stuart Garrard (*The source*, 146).

**(Allow approximately 5 minutes for this)**

Hardly a day goes by without some news which shocks us and causes us to question someone's behaviour.

**Read Luke 13:1-9**
Jesus is brought news of an atrocity carried out by the Roman soldiers

acting on the orders of Pilate. It was almost as if he were being asked, 'How much more evidence to you need before you condemn the Romans for what they do?'

To the Jews, the whole concept of the 'Messiah' or 'Saviour' was that God would establish his kingdom on earth. Many believed that Jesus was going to force the Romans out of Israel and a new order, or government, would take their place. The Essenes, in particular, trained for the day when God's kingdom would be established by force. Another collection of groups was known as the Zealots, who thought that God might need a bit of a hand when it came to sorting out the Romans. Several other small groups existed, including one called the Sicarii (dagger men), who carried out assassinations and really wound the Roman authorities up.

So the people were expecting Jesus to say, 'Yeah, let's give those Romans a real hiding.' Instead of inciting them to action, Jesus suggested that the people look at the situation from another perspective. Firstly, he wanted everyone to understand that the people who had been killed were not being punished by God for being dodgy characters. And secondly, he wanted to get across the idea that everyone is capable of behaving in a way or committing acts that some other people would find horrifying.

In Luke 13:5, Jesus puts forward the view that the people should hate the sin, or crime, but not hate the person involved. The story of the fig tree is one way of suggesting that we need to be patient and give a person time to regret what they've done and turn to God. Forgiveness is an easy word to say but an extremely difficult thing to do. Jesus is warning against creating a 'goodies' and 'baddies' list because everyone is capable of doing the wrong thing. Change is a heart attitude and not an act of revenge.

Ask the group if they have heard of any news or events recently which have made them feel angry or powerless. Discuss some of the atrocities or natural disasters which have occurred in various parts of the world.

- What do the group feel about these situations?
- Is anyone to blame?
- What should happen to the people involved?

Discuss some local or personal issues which cause the group to feel similar emotions to those provoked by what they've just discussed. Why did these events happen? Could they have been avoided?

Give each member of the group a piece of paper and a pen. Ask each of them to write a sentence or two about a situation which they feel strongly about or one in which they may have been involved. When they have finished, fold the pieces of paper and place them in a pile in the centre of the room.

**(Allow 5 minutes)**

Suggest to the group that they should now spend a few moments thinking about the situation they've just written on the paper. While they are quiet, read the following prayer:

Lord,
I've gone through every emotion in the dictionary.
I've shouted until my throat hurts.
My head aches with the thoughts
    of senseless violence,
    of mindless actions
    that have robbed people
    of their hopes, their dreams, their lives.
I can't pretend to understand
    or find an answer
    to the jigsaw of events
    that froze a moment in time
    for ever.
Tears sometimes say more
    than mere words can express.
A cry from the heart
    speaks more wisdom
    than a thousand wise men.
But all I can say is
    I don't understand, Lord.
All I can pray is
    that somehow,
    for all those involved,
    you would bring peace
    and understanding,
    while I place my life
    in your hands.
Keep me safe, keep me willing
    to hear your voice and your heart.

# A man's gotta do . . .

## Luke 13:31-35: Jesus and Herod

**Equipment:**
clip-on clothes-pegs
flipchart
pair of scissors
sticky tape
music and lyrics

Divide the group into three categories: Grabbers, Givers and Goodies. Distribute the clip-on clothes-pegs so that every group member has the same number of pegs and ask everyone to put the pegs anywhere on their clothes as long as they are visible (the more pegs each member has the better).

At a given signal, the three groups go around and behave as their name implies. The 'Grabbers' try and take as many pegs as they can and put them onto their clothing, the 'Givers' simply offer their pegs to anyone and the 'Goodies' try and take the pegs that the 'Grabbers' have taken and give them back to the original owner!

It might be advisable to suggest that you are not liable for any torn clothing!

**(Allow 10 minutes for this activity)**

Sometimes, feelings of anger, frustration or confusion can distract us from our intended aim or destination. It can be difficult to keep going when everything seems to be against you.

Try having a look at 'Called to a battle' by Noel and Tricia Richards (*The source,* 61) or 'We shall stand' by Graham Kendrick (*The source*, 556).

**(Allow approximately 5 minutes for this)**

How would we react if what we were doing provoked a threat on our lives? Would we decide that it might be better to live a while longer and take a rain-check on our actions or would we shrug our shoulders and get on with what we intended to do?

**Read Luke 13:31-35**

Jesus and the Pharisees had not seen eye to eye during the past few months. Some of them had bad-mouthed Jesus and he'd had a few choice words to say about them and their 'religious' behaviour.

The Jews themselves had defined seven behavioural categories of Pharisee. They called one category the 'Shoulder' Pharisees, because whatever good deed or act of kindness that they did, they made sure everyone knew about it. There were the 'Hang on a minute' Pharisees who played the game of 'put it off' whenever it came to helping someone or parting with money. Another category were the 'Bruised' Pharisees who thought that looking at a woman was sinful and so closed their eyes whenever they saw a female. Walking into solid objects was a very frequent occurrence! One category always walked as if they were carrying a huge weight on their shoulders. They believed that walking with a stoop was a sign of humility; other people thought they were just plain stupid.

One group of Pharisees kept a diary of their good deeds and used this as a sort of bargaining account with God. Perhaps it went something like: 'God, I've done three good deeds this week and now it's my turn, OK?' Another category were those Pharisees who believed that at any moment God would get really angry with them and so they went around continually looking behind them (that category is the 'Timid' Pharisees). And finally, there were those Pharisees who genuinely believed that doing acts of charity and being honest with God was the best way to follow and worship God.

So, when some Pharisees came to Jesus and warned him of Herod's threat to kill him, it could have been difficult to try and guess what the Pharisees were up to. Were they really concerned about the threat to Jesus, or did they think they were doing a good deed by warning him? Did it count as a 'tick' in the 'act of kindness' box, or did they see Herod's threat as part of God's anger for some reason? Jesus could have spent all day trying to sort out why, and for whose benefit, these Pharisees had come to warn him. But rather than waste time, he decided that he had a task to complete and nothing was going to stop him. Even though Jesus knew for certain that he was going to his death, he was determined to do things his way (which was God's way) and it didn't matter what people might say or do.

Remind the group of the game they played at the beginning of the session. Discuss some of the following questions:

- How did they feel during the game? Angry, amused, or totally bewildered?
- Did the game seem pointless?
- What did they think of the role they were asked to perform (Grabber, Giver or Goodie)?
- Did they feel like changing roles at any time? Why?

Can the group think of any circumstances or situations that compare with the game? For instance, do they know people who are always on the take? Or people who give their time or money for charity? Can the game help us understand the feelings of other people?

Ask the group to suggest words which indicate how they felt during the game. Whether they felt awkward, daft, annoyed, puzzled or frustrated, each of these words can make us question what we believe we should be doing. Write the words onto a flipchart.

**(Allow 5 minutes)**

Place the flipchart in the centre of the room or cut the words out and stick them around the room. Ask the group to think about any situation or problem where they feel unable to do what they believe is the right thing. While the group are quiet, read the following:

Proverbs 3:1-6.
My child, remember my teachings and instructions
    and obey them completely.
They will help you live a long and prosperous life.
Let love and loyalty always show like a necklace,
    and write them in your mind.
God and people will like you and consider you a success.
With all your heart you must trust the Lord
    and not in your own judgement.
Always let him lead you,
    and he will clear the road for you to follow.

# So what are you gonna do?

## Luke 15:1-3,11-32: Two sons

**Equipment:**
large cardboard box
four or five smaller boxes
tape, glue and paper-clips
straws, pipe-cleaners, bamboo canes and thin wire
toy car or ball
stones
basket
flipchart
music and lyrics

Divide the group into four or five teams. Place the large box in the centre of the room. Arrange the smaller boxes in a circle with the large box in the centre. Each team is given a collection of tape, glue, paper-clips, straws, pipe-cleaners, canes and wire. The object is to build a bridge from the smaller box across to the large box in the centre (the distance between the large box and smaller ones depends on the space available and how difficult you want to make the task).

The winning team is the one whose bridge can support the toy car or the ball as it travels from the small box to the large box.

- How did the groups organise themselves?
- Were they successful?
- Why?
- What problems occurred?

**(Allow 10 minutes for this activity)**

Building bridges offers a lot of insights into individual and group behaviour.

Take a look at 'Oh, I was made for this' by Graham Kendrick (*The source*, 389) or 'Did you feel the mountains tremble?' by Martin Smith (*The source*, 80).

**(Allow approximately 5 minutes for this)**

Building bridges takes a lot of effort and can often prove to be more difficult than we ever imagined.

**Read Luke 15:1-3, 11-32.**

Jesus gives us a story-line any soap opera would be proud of. Under Jewish law the eldest son was entitled to two thirds of his father's property and the youngest son was given a third. Sometimes the father could give his sons their inheritance early if he wanted to retire from running his affairs and take it easy. But in this instance, the younger son actually says, 'I wish you were dead.' Things must have been pretty rough for the son to feel like this. Perhaps, as the younger son, he felt he wasn't given enough respect or responsibility. He might even have been jealous of the fact that his elder brother was going to get twice as much of the inheritance as he was. There are many reasons why families argue, fall out and say things they later wish they hadn't.

In the story, the young son allowed the money to slip through his hands and he was left hoping that the pigs would leave him a few crumbs to eat. For a Jew, the pig was about as welcome as a chocolate gâteau at a weight-watchers' convention.

The younger son soon realised that he had lost more than he had ever gained by turning his back on his father and decided to go home and ask to become one of his father's farm workers. As soon as his father saw him coming, he ran to meet him (the father running from his property to greet his son wasn't a normal action in Jewish society).

Once back home the young son was treated far differently from what he had expected. He was given a robe, which meant the same as giving someone honour and respect. Then he was given a ring, which signified authority. Next he was given shoes, which were a symbol of freedom and finally, a feast was prepared. Father and son were reconciled, brought back together, not back to where they were when the argument began, but to a new place, a position where the son was given more than he could ever hope for.

In contrast, the elder brother lost the plot completely. He was annoyed at his father's actions, and refused to be reconciled to his brother. Everyone within the family had been affected by the young son's actions but the father had chosen to welcome his son back with open arms. Perhaps if the father (God) decides to throw a party we should all take part in the celebration and not question his judgement. In other words, if God forgives, who are we to argue?

Ask the group to suggest situations that they've experienced where arguments have caused people to feel separated from those they once felt close to.

- How did it happen?
- What were the causes?
- Have the people concerned dealt with the problem?
- How was it resolved?

You might have to be sensitive to some of the issues or the fact that some of the group may feel too awkward or shy to talk personally. It may prove easier to discuss ways of avoiding conflict within a group or family. Ask group members to suggest a list of recommended actions or behaviour which either avoid conflict or bring people back together.

**(Allow 5 minutes)**

Give each of the group members a small pebble or stone. Ask them to think of someone close to them who is experiencing a problem within their family. Place a basket in the centre of the room and after the group have spent a few moments in thought, ask them to place the stone in the basket. The collected stones represent everyone who is having a difficult time at the moment. If the group agree, you might like to write names or initials of the people involved on a piece of paper and place them on a notice board as a prayer reminder.

While everyone is quiet, read the following prayer:

Lord,
  it's often difficult
  to know who's right and who's wrong.
Just as it takes two to argue,
  it takes two to agree
  to build the bridge
  which will join two islands
  that have been separated
  by an ocean of misunderstanding.
Please help us to learn
  how to build bridges,
  no matter how far
  or how wide
  the gap.
Help us to be willing
  to realise the loneliness
  of anger, of hurt and of damaged pride,
  so that we can be a continent of hope
  and not a cluster of islands in a raging sea.

# Causing a bit of a stir!

## John 2:13-22: Jesus in the Temple

**Equipment:**
pen and paper for each group member
large sheet of paper and marker
music and lyrics
wastepaper basket

Ask the group to think about all the things that make them angry – really angry. For instance, someone leaving their dirty socks on the table, or borrowing your toothbrush without asking.

Suggest to the group that they choose one of the things which makes them angry and write it on their piece of paper. Chat about the 'angry-making things', write some of them on the large sheet of paper and display it where everyone can see it. The group should keep their sheet of paper for later. **(Allow 10 minutes for this activity.)**

Ask the group to have a listen to 'God's House' by Three Crosses, from the album *Three Crosses*. Alternatively, have a look at 'Our God is an awesome God' by Noel and Tricia Richards (*The source*, 418) or 'Let the same mind' by Graham Kendrick (*The source new songs*, 35). Try and have a copy of the lyrics available. **(Allow approximately 5 minutes.)**

Discuss the chosen piece of music. What did the lyrics have to say? What was their meaning?

**Read John 2:13-22**
The Passover was an extremely important feast for the Jews. The law stated that every adult male who lived within fifteen miles of Jerusalem must attend the feast.

When the male Jews arrived in Jerusalem and visited the Temple, they were asked to pay a temple tax equal to an average day's wage. This tax was to ensure that the temple rituals were carried out each day. But the tax had to be paid in special Jewish currency. Any other coins were considered 'unclean' and not acceptable. To help the pilgrims offer the 'correct' coins, a group of money changers was available in the Temple precincts. The money changers charged the equivalent of one day's wage to exchange the pilgrims' coins;

that's the wages for two days paid out already and the feast hasn't even started!

The next stage was to offer a sacrifice at the Temple. This sacrifice was an offering of thanks for a safe journey or some other event in the life of the pilgrim. A pilgrim could take their own animal into the Temple for sacrifice or buy an animal from one of the traders outside the Temple. A small animal would cost the equivalent of one day's wages. But the temple rules stated that a sacrificial animal must be perfect. So, any animal that was brought into the Temple was inspected for a small fee – about a quarter of a day's wages.

It was almost certain that any animal bought outside the Temple would be declared 'impure'. This meant the pilgrim would have to buy one of the 'pure' animals from the stall holders inside the Temple. A small animal which cost a quarter of a day's wages outside the Temple would cost the same as twenty days' wages from a stall holder inside the Temple! So, for a quick trip to the Temple, it has cost approximately twenty-two days' wages. Some feast!

If you were rich, the cost of visiting the Temple was not a major problem. If you were poor it was a major problem. No wonder Jesus was so angry about this social injustice. More importantly, most people would see no more of God's house than the market where they got ripped off. What did this say about God? It certainly gave the impression that God could be bought and that having faith in God was like a market place, the best deals on offer to those who could afford it!

Jesus found some rope and made a whip. He then created a real stir by chasing everyone out of the Temple while shouting, 'Don't make my Father's house a market place.'

Jesus was angry because the impression that people got of God was so wrong. The injustice and trading that took place created an unnatural distance between God and his people. It also gave the impression that God and his priests were in the faith business for profit. Jesus knew that before long the greatest sacrifice in history would be made. A sacrifice which was totally 'pure' was to be made at no cost to God's people. He alone was going to bear the cost. Jesus had every right to be angry!

Look at those 'angry' statements which were written and displayed earlier.

- What can the group do to stop the 'angry-making' things getting at them?
- Can they suggest ways which would reduce the possibility of getting angry?
- Are some things just too much trouble?

Ask the group to take the piece of paper on which they have written their 'angry' statement. Without looking at it again, screw the piece of paper up into a ball. Keep hold of the 'ball' for a moment.

**(Allow 5 minutes for this task)**

Place a wastepaper basket in the centre of the room. Ask the group to place their paper into the basket. Once this has been done, pray the following prayer:

Lord, if I think too much
there are so many things
which make me really, really angry.
So angry that they make my head feel
crowded, heavy, too full to think.
I can't help looking at everything else
through angry eyes.
I don't want to feel like this,
as if my life is one long angry statement.
Lord, take this anger from me,
help me to do what is right in your eyes.
Help me to look beyond the anger
and see someone who you love,
even though they can really get under my skin at times! Amen.

# What's that smell?

## John 12:1-8: At Bethany

**Equipment:**
range of small bottles
various coloured liquids
flipchart
music and lyrics

Pour the liquids into the bottles. Try using a variety of liquids which have a distinctive smell, e.g. disinfectant, perfume, tea, coffee, orange, water. You might like to make some of the 'aromas' more interesting by adding some noxious as well as pleasant smells!

Organise a number of volunteers from the group and blindfold each of them. One by one arrange for each volunteer to smell the liquids and ask them to guess what is contained within each bottle. As a special treat, ask each volunteer for a number (if there are eight bottles, numbers between 1 and 8). Whichever number they choose, they are allowed to have a drop of the liquid from the chosen bottle placed behind their ear!

**(Allow 10 minutes for this activity)**

Apprehension and sometimes annoyance can often blind us to seeing what is really in front of our noses.

Have a look at 'You laid aside your majesty' by Noel Richards (*The source*, 601) or 'At your feet we fall' by David Fellingham (*The source*, 35).

**(Allow approximately 5 minutes for this)**

It's only too easy to think that who we are and what we have isn't worth a great deal.

**Read John 12:1-8**

Jesus had gone to Bethany, to the house of Simon the Leper, for a meal. Martha, Mary and Lazarus were most likely the children of Simon. The meal was to be a leisurely dinner, a time to enjoy eating, drinking and good company.

The meal had been prepared especially for Jesus after his extremely busy time teaching and healing all around the area. The sight of Lazarus at the table would have made the meal a special occasion. Lazarus (formerly known as dead Lazarus!) was a close friend and Jesus must have taken real pleasure in raising him from the dead.

Everyone would have known that the meal was a special occasion but not everyone would have been able to say why it was so special. Jesus knew that these were his last few days of freedom and being with his disciples and close friends would have been particularly important for him. The disciples would have known that things were 'hotting up' but even they might not have been able to say precisely what was going to happen. To Mary, Martha and Lazarus it was enough to have their close friend spend some time with them.

Martha seems to have been the practical person, the one who knew how to make people feel comfortable and catered for. She offered her skills in the kitchen as an expression of her love towards Jesus. Mary expressed her love in a different way.

The washing of feet was a normal courtesy before a meal. Mary's actions were significant for three reasons. First, the perfume that Mary poured on Jesus' feet was expensive and quite probably irreplaceable, given the cost. Second, it was usually traditional, and a sign of honour, to use oil or perfume to anoint someone's head. By anointing Jesus' feet Mary was showing her humility by not claiming the honour of anointing Jesus' head. And third, Mary wiped Jesus' feet with her hair. At the time, no respectable woman would appear in public with her hair loose. By using her hair to wipe his feet of Jesus, Mary was setting aside tradition and respectability in her desire to express her love for Jesus, regardless of what people thought of her.

In their different ways both Mary and Martha gave Jesus an expression of their love. No one objected to Martha's gift of food as everyone would have shared in the meal and enjoyed the food. Mary's gift was personal and only for Jesus.

We each have our own, individual ways of expressing how we feel and what we consider precious. Every expression is relevant and special. Just because some acts are highly visible and make an impact immediately doesn't mean that other forms of expression are less important or meaningful. Each of us is unique and important to God. The most important thing is the expression of our hearts, not what other people think of us.

Ask the group to think of the things that other people do for them which help make their lives comfortable, happy or bearable. Write some of the comments on the flipchart. What about some of the things people do that we take for granted, e.g washing clothes, tidying bedrooms, preparing meals? List all the ways in which people contribute to our daily lives. Now, turn the question around and ask the group to consider ways in which they contribute to other people's well-being. Underline the actions which come into both categories – ways in which the group members both give and receive.

**(Allow 5 minutes)**

Place the flipchart in the centre of the room and ask the group to think about some of the ways in which people help them. While the group are quiet, read the following prayer:

Lord,
    you'll have to speak up,
    I can't hear you very well.
The sound of my own voice
    is almost deafening
    with a dustbin
    over my head.
It's not the best place to be,
    underneath a container for rubbish.
But perhaps it's the best place
    for the dustbin.
I wasn't pushed,
    I didn't stumble or trip.
I'm sitting here
    by choice
    because it's how I feel
    about myself.
Excuse me,
    what was that you said?
You want to come and join me?
Surely you can find a better place to be.
Pardon?
You can't think of anywhere better
    than here with me?
Hang on a minute, I'm coming out.
There's not enough room for two
    and anyway, I feel much better now there's you and me.

# To die is to live

## John 12:20-33: Jesus predicts his death

**Equipment:**
sliced loaf
butter and jam
knife and small plate
music and lyrics
penlight torch

Have the loaf, butter and jam on display as the group arrive. Announce to the group that you have recently discovered the delights of eating bread and jam; you can't think of anything better to eat for breakfast, lunch, tea and supper. In fact, so obsessed are you with bread and jam that you have given up all other forms of food. But you have decided that this obsession is possibly a bit too silly. After all, jam every day? You need the group to help you out. Can they suggest some different toppings for the bread?

Make a list of their suggestions. Now tell the group that a thought has just struck you. Given the additives that are put into some bread and the different types of bread (white, wholemeal, granary and so on), you think it might be safer to buy the wheat grain before the farmer has sown it! Can you still serve the grain with the toppings the group suggested?

The group should tell you that the wheat grain has to be planted, has to germinate, grow and be harvested, ground into flour and then baked. Ask them why all this has to take place.

**(Allow 10 minutes for this activity)**

Have a look at 'Over the mountains and the sea' by Martin Smith (*The source*, 421) or 'Open the eyes of my heart' by Paul Baloche (*The source 2*, 926). You might like to use a different piece of music with a similar theme. Have a copy of the lyrics available if possible.

**(Allow approximately 5 minutes)**

Discuss the piece of music with the group. Did the lyrics help the group think about life and how we can make the most of it?

**Read John 12:20-33**

Jesus is speaking in Jerusalem at the time of the Passover (a special Jewish festival). A large crowd had gathered to welcome Jesus into Jerusalem. The crowd had shouted, 'God bless the King of Israel!' Expectations were running high. Miracles had been witnessed, people healed, demons sent packing and the dead raised! Now Jesus declares, 'The time has come for the Son of Man to be given his glory.'

His followers must have given the thumbs up to this statement. About time! Just what we need! We'll show those Romans and those religious snobs in the Temple. You can imagine the scene.

But then, before any of this can really sink in, Jesus tells one of his odd stories. 'I tell you for certain that a grain of wheat that falls on the ground will never be more than one grain unless it dies. But if it dies, it will produce lots of wheat.' (John 12:24)

What is this bloke on about? Can you imagine the followers' faces now?

One moment Jesus is talking about being glorified and the next about grains of wheat dying! Jesus was telling his disciples that his mission was to die! He was to die to bring glory to the Father and be the sacrifice for humankind. Through his death would come life for everyone.

But Jesus asks his disciples to follow his example: to die to their old lifestyle and allow a totally new life to emerge. His followers must have thought that this was an impossible concept to grasp. To live you must first die? The grain of wheat was simply a grain of wheat until it was 'buried' in the ground. Only when the grain of wheat had 'died' did it develop its potential to grow and become much more than it was before. Only when this process has taken place does the wheat bring life to other people (by being made into flour and then into bread).

If Jesus had been selfish and refused to suffer and die then we could never have a real relationship with God. Jesus gave his life so that everyone could live to have this relationship with God.

We have a choice, whether to hold on to our lives as they are, or give our lives to God. We have the opportunity to become what God has intended for us or to remain inward looking and keep our eyes on the ground. Just as Jesus was lifted up to die, so we can lift up our eyes to see that through his death we can have life.

We have a choice . . .

Discuss with the group what Jesus means about life and death.

- What makes it difficult for us to give our lives to God?
- What fears do we have?
- How do we know that God wants the best for us?

**(Allow 5 minutes for this task)**

If it is possible, make the room dark. Shine a small penlight torch directly on the ceiling above the group. Ask the group to lift their eyes to look at the light. While they do this, read the following prayer:

Jesus, at times it's really difficult,
really difficult to understand what you mean.
It's even more difficult to do what you say,
even when we understand.
It's not easy.
I know it's about faith, it's about trust.
Easy to say, but not easy to put into practice.
As I lift my eyes
allow me to see what you meant
by dying to live;
by giving to receive.
Thank you for my choice.
Help me to use my choice,
rather than ignore it.
You died for me to live.
What more can I say? Amen.

# Jesus finds a donkey

## John 12:12-16: Jesus enters Jerusalem

**Equipment:**
flipchart and marker pen
music and lyrics
palm cross
paper and pens

Announce to the group that you are going to a party during the week and you are a bit unsure what to wear. Can the group make any suggestions? Ask the group what they would wear if they were going to a really smart party. Make a list of the types of outfits and accessories. What kind of vehicle would each member of the group like to arrive in at the party? Would they invite the press and photographers to record the event of the year? Which magazines or newspapers would they like to see themselves in?

**(Allow 10 minutes for this activity)**

A lot of people make up their minds about who and what we are from the way we look. But things are not always what they seem.

Take a look at 'The happy song' by Martin Smith (*The source*, 200) or 'O sacred King' by Matt Redman (*The source new songs*, 50). You can use a different piece of music with a similar theme. Try and have a copy of the lyrics available.

**(Allow approximately 5 minutes)**

Discuss the piece of music with the group. What did the lyrics have to say about Jesus and/or God?

**Read John 12:12-16**

The Passover Feast was an important part of Jewish culture. At least once in their life each male Jew would try and attend the Feast in Jerusalem. There would have been several hundred thousand people gathered in Jerusalem. The atmosphere would have been one of great expectancy and excitement.

Jesus rode into Jerusalem to be met by a huge crowd of people all shouting and waving palm branches. It must have been an amazing sight!

Immediately before arriving in Jerusalem, Jesus had performed yet another miracle by raising Lazarus from the dead. The chief priests were already plotting how to get rid of Jesus. They were also trying to figure out how to kill Lazarus!

Two main features of the entry into Jerusalem stand out:

Firstly, Jesus rode into Jerusalem as a wanted man. Not wanted as a liberator or saviour by the priests but wanted by them as a criminal. Even the disciples were taken up with the idea that Jesus had at last come to claim his place as King of the Jews. The people greeted Jesus with a cry of 'Hosanna' or 'hooray', which roughly translates as 'please save us'. This was a shout of praise to God but it would have made the chief priests even angrier than before, as it was also a shout acknowledging that Jesus was in some way connected with God; worse, that he was a 'saviour'!

Secondly, Jesus rode into Jerusalem on a donkey! This act fulfils the prophecy from the Old Testament book Zechariah (9:9-10). Zechariah writes that everyone in Jerusalem should celebrate and shout 'your King has won a victory and he is coming to you . . . riding on a donkey' (verse 9). We may not think that riding a donkey gives the impression of a king! In Old Testament times, if a king were going to war, he would ride a horse. But if the king rode a donkey it meant he came in peace. Jesus made a significant statement. He rode into Jerusalem as a king of peace; not to liberate the world by force but by peace.

Even though Jesus knew that he was considered a threat to the chief priests (see verse 19) and that he would die a criminal's death, he rode a donkey to make the most profound statement.

God didn't send his Son into the world to condemn its people but to save them (see John 3:17). The Prince of Peace rode a donkey knowing that he would die a violent death at the hands of soldiers for a crime he didn't commit.

Ask the group to consider the entry of Jesus into Jerusalem. Picture the scene with the excited crowds all waving palm branches and shouting.

- What do they think the disciples and followers of Jesus thought?
- Did they think a major change was about to take place?
- Did they think that Jesus was going to cause a revolt against the Romans?

**(Allow 5 minutes for this task)**

Place a palm cross in the centre of the room. Give each member of the group a piece of paper and a pen. Ask them to write on the piece of paper an issue or situation that is causing trouble or giving them concern. The issue or situation may or may not involve the group member directly. When each member has written an issue or situation which they are concerned about, ask them to fold the paper and place it by the palm cross. When everyone has placed their piece of paper by the cross, read the following prayer:

Lord, trouble seems to have a habit of getting under my skin.
It itches and aggravates,
    and the more I scratch it, the more it itches.
How does trouble find me?
I certainly don't go looking for it,
    it seems to find me wherever I am.
It's not always my fault,
    well, sometimes maybe, but not every time!
Please help me to see things your way,
    because my way sometimes misses the point
    or makes the trouble worse!
I need to see things your way,
    because I have the knack
    of sometimes missing the obvious
    or making up my mind
    without knowing all the facts.
You seemed to know what you were doing
    on the way into Jerusalem.
Even though others thought it odd
    that a king should ride a donkey.
But you had other thoughts in mind,
    beyond what could be imagined
    by your closest friends.
Prince of Peace, take my troubles
    and bring your peace instead. Amen.

# A bit of a do

## Luke 22:14-23: The Lord's Supper

**Equipment:**
pack of playing cards
bread and wine/juice
music and lyrics

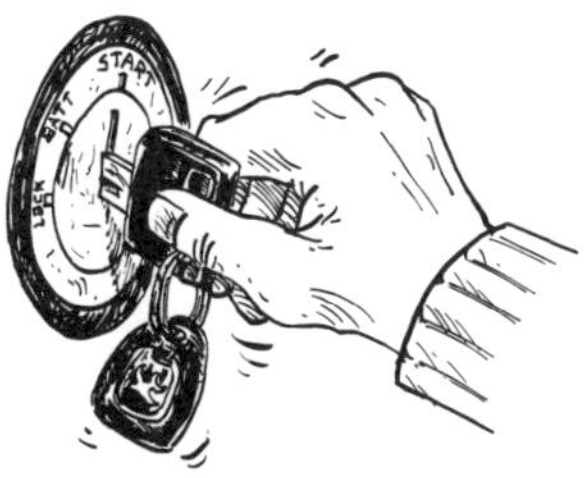

Select sufficient cards for each member of the group to have one card. Make sure you include either the Queen of Clubs or the Queen of Spades, but not both. Shuffle the cards and distribute one card to each member of the group. The group must not show their card to any other member of the group. The game is simple. The holder of the black queen has to eliminate the other members of the group by winking at them once. The person winked at counts to ten, then places their card in front of them and say 'I'm out'. They must not identify the person who winked at them. If a member of the group thinks they know who's 'winking' then they are allowed to accuse them. If they are wrong, the accuser is out of the game. The game continues until everyone is 'out' or the eliminator is discovered.

**(Allow 10 minutes for this activity)**

It's infuriating trying to sort out the innocent and the guilty.

Take a look at 'We do not presume' by Andy Piercy *(The source*, 545) or 'Here is bread' by Graham Kendrick (*The source*, 163).

**(Allow approximately 5 minutes for this)**

Another meal but this time the mood is sombre.

**Read Luke 22:14-23**

The Passover meal was a celebration of the release of the Israelites from slavery in Egypt (see Exodus 12-13). Jesus brought his disciples together to share in his last Passover meal, which the disciples understood was a special meal because everyone in Jerusalem, and many visitors to the city, celebrated the Passover. For Jesus, this meal held more significance than the disciples appreciated.

The relationship between Jesus and the religious authorities had become tense. He had challenged their traditions and thinking and they were worried he was becoming too popular. The disciples were also aware of the tension but they seemed confident that Jesus had everything under control. Jesus did have everything under control, but not in the way the disciples thought.

On the night of the original 'Passover' the angel of death killed every first-born son but *passed over* the homes where the lintels of the doors had been smeared with the blood of a lamb. Jesus had already been referred to as the 'Lamb of God' (see John 1:29).

During his meal with the disciples, Jesus took the unleavened bread (made without yeast as a reminder of how the Israelites had to escape from Egypt as quickly as possible – there hadn't been any time to wait for the dough to rise). The bread was a symbol, recalling a significant event. Jesus took the bread, broke it and told his disciples that the bread represented his body, to be broken as a sacrifice. Next, Jesus took the wine, another symbol, and drank it. The wine was to act as a reminder of Jesus' blood, which again represented a sacrifice.

The death and sacrifice of Jesus was the only way in which a relationship with God could be restored. The symbols of the bread and the wine are constant reminders that we have continuous access to God because of the sacrifice of Jesus.

Place the bread and the wine/juice on a table in front of the group. Can the group think of other symbols that remind us of events or special occasions? For example cross, dove, fish. Discuss the importance of symbols.

- Why do we need symbols?
- Would we forget without symbols to remind us?

**(Allow 5 minutes)**

Leave the bread and the wine/juice on the table and ask the group to be quiet while you read the following:

Psalm 107:1-9.
Shout praises to the Lord!
He is good to us, and his love never fails.
Everyone the Lord has rescued from trouble
    should praise him.
Everyone he has brought from the east and the west,
    the north and the south.
Some of you were lost in the scorching desert,
    far from a town.
You were hungry and thirsty and about to give up.
You were in serious trouble,
    but you prayed to the Lord, and he rescued you.
Straight away he brought you to a town.
You should praise the Lord for his love

and for the wonderful things he does for all of us.
To everyone who is thirsty, he gives something to drink;
to everyone who is hungry
he gives good things to eat.

# You must be seeing things!

## Luke 24:1-12: Jesus is alive

**Equipment:**
flipchart
glue or tacks
assorted pictures
pens and paper
seed from a plant
music and lyrics

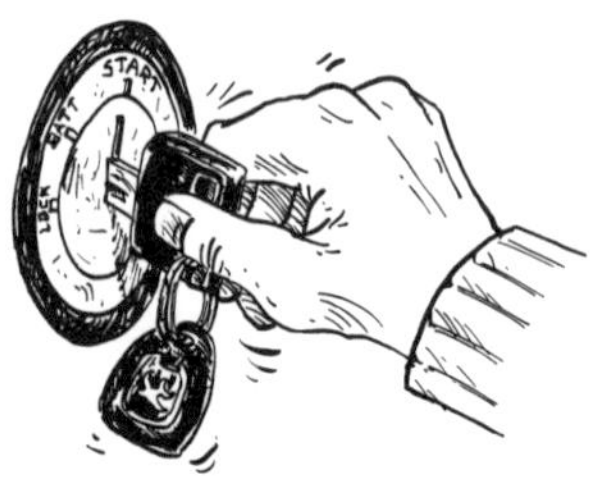

Select a variety of pictures taken from a wide range of magazines and/or newspapers. Cut out a portion of the picture so that the image is incomplete (remember to keep a note of what the picture was originally). Stick or glue the images onto the flipchart and number each image.

Distribute the pens and paper to the group and ask them to guess what the original picture was. The person with the most correct answers is the winner.

**(Allow 10 minutes for this activity)**

Images are open to our interpretation. It isn't always as easy as we think to identify even familiar images from a small portion or a strange angle.

Have a look at 'I will love you for the cross' by Matt Redman and Beth Vickers (*Re:source 2000*, 6) or 'Nothing shall separate us' by Noel and Tricia Richards (*The source*, 377).

**(Allow approximately 5 minutes)**

Newspapers thrive on reports of strange sightings and unexplained phenomena.

**Read Luke 24:1-12**

It was extremely early on Sunday morning. It was still dark although the sun was just starting to signal its arrival for the day. Mary and several other women went to the tomb of Jesus to complete the last functions of the burial ceremony. The spices they took with them would have been a mixture of myrrh and aloes which acted as a sort of disinfectant and deodorant. It would have been a very sad occasion for the women. After three hectic yet incredible years, where Jesus had literally changed people's lives, the end had come. The final act of putting spices on the dead body was almost like closing a book; it was finished.

Jesus had used these very same words a couple of days earlier as he had hung on the cross: 'It is finished.' But his idea of 'finished' was very different from that of the women who came to his tomb. What Jesus had struggled for and eventually died for was finished. Stage One was complete and now Stage Two was about to begin.

When the women arrived at the tomb, the heavy circular stone had been moved, the tomb was open. Inside the tomb, the body had vanished. Various questions must have gone through the women's minds. What could have happened? Who could have taken the body? The women's thoughts were occupied with the practical side of things: who, what, where? They'd seen Jesus die – that was it, over and done.

In the gloom two men appeared. Their clothes shone in the darkness. The sight must have been frightening. The women were already concerned about the loss of the body and now here was something else to think about. The response from the two men was incredible. Why were the women looking where dead people were buried? Well, what else are you supposed to find in a graveyard? Then the amazing statement: 'Jesus isn't here, he's alive!'

The women ran back to the disciples and told them what they had and hadn't seen. The Greek word, which the disciples used to describe the women's report is one more often used by ancient Greek doctors to define someone who is 'babbling', someone who has a fever or is insane. The women's mixture of amazement and excitement didn't seem to make any impression on the disciples who must have been more interested in what was for breakfast.

Only Peter, who had denied Jesus three times, had the courage to check the story out. He also returned confused and wondering what had happened. Now it wasn't so much who had done it, but why?

Ask the group what words they think would describe the thoughts and feelings of the women when they went to the tomb of Jesus. Write them up on the flipchart. Then ask them for words to describe the thoughts and feelings of the disciples after the women had come back with their report.

- Do any of these words describe our thoughts or the way we feel about God, Jesus, the Holy Spirit?
- Is there a problem with us having these kinds of thoughts?
- If even the people who had known Jesus well could feel that way, then isn't it only reasonable for us to have the same thoughts and feelings whenever we try to understand what God wants with us?

**(Allow 5 minutes)**

Place the seed on a table where everybody can see it. Can anyone identify the plant from the seed? With difficulty or not at all! Only when the plant becomes established can we really be certain what it is and what we can use it for. We have to be patient.

Our life is similar to the seed. Where we are going and what we are going to do in the future are questions we would all like to know the answers to. It's possibly a good job that we can't always! We need to trust that God knows what he's doing.

Ask the group to be quiet while you read the following:

Psalm 62:5-8.
Only God gives inward peace, and I depend on him.
God alone is the mighty rock that keeps me safe,
    and he is the fortress where I feel secure.
God saves me and honours me.
He is that mighty rock where I find safety.
Trust God, my friends,
    and always tell him each one of your concerns.
God is our place of safety.

# Lock that door!

## John 20:19-31: Jesus appears to his disciples

**Equipment:**
card
pen and paper
candle
music and lyrics

You will need an even number of pieces of card. On one piece of card draw a series of interlocking shapes, similar to a puzzle. Copy the 'puzzle' onto a second card. Taking another card, draw a different 'puzzle' and again copy the 'puzzle' onto another piece of card. Repeat the process until you have used all the cards. On the 'original' set of cards, cut out the interlocking shapes leaving a completed copy for each 'puzzle'.

Divide the group into pairs. Have the pairs sit back to back so that they cannot see each other's 'puzzle'. One of the partners has the copy of the 'puzzle' while the other has the cut-out pieces. The partner with the copy 'puzzle' tries to describe each piece of the 'puzzle' and where to place it.

What difficulties did the group have completing the 'puzzles'?

**(Allow 10 minutes for this activity)**

During the previous activity some feelings of confusion may have crept into the proceedings!

Take a look at 'I'm learning to love you' by Paul Oakley (*Re:source 2000*, 4) or 'Though I feel afraid' by Ian White (*The source*, 522).

**(Allow approximately 5 minutes)**



Feelings of confusion and fear often make a situation appear hopeless.

**Read John 20:19-31**

It had been a horrendous few days for the disciples. Everything they had believed in and hoped for appeared to have gone for ever. All sorts of rumours were doing the rounds about what had happened to Jesus and what would happen to the disciples if the Jewish leaders got hold of them!

Confusion was the flavour of the day as the disciples gathered together in a room. Fear of being caught by the authorities drove them to lock the door. So many different thoughts must have been going through their minds. Why had the people suddenly turned against them? What more did Jesus have to do to prove who he was? What would happen to the disciples now? Where could they go? Was it possible for them to return to their former jobs and carry on as if nothing had happened? Questions, questions, fear and confusion, but no answers.

The feelings of dejection and hopelessness must have coloured their thoughts. Each of the disciples had experienced so much and seen so many amazing things happen that they must have been wishing for a miracle.

They hardly had time to blink before Jesus appeared in the middle of the room. The disciples probably thought that they'd all gone completely bonkers. This couldn't be happening, could it?

Jesus approached them with an everyday greeting: 'Peace be to you.' This carried a more significant meaning than simply 'I hope you don't get into trouble'! – although keeping out of trouble must have been just what the disciples wanted. The greeting means: 'May God give you every good thing.'

The disciples may have been a bit sceptical at first. You can imagine their first reaction to be, 'Yeah, we could do with a few good things, like how to get the authorities off our backs', but their scepticism was short-lived after Jesus had showed them his hands and side. The disciples may still have felt a little confused but at least they didn't feel as if they were on their own any more.

Although Jesus had explained to the disciples what was going to happen, when things began to get tough the disciples couldn't help feeling confused and frightened. Jesus had promised that he wouldn't just leave them to get on with life on their own.

It's never easy to feel confident when situations get a bit sticky. All too often we can feel as if we're up to our necks in it and completely on our own. But Jesus has given his word that he will never leave us to try and sort things out by ourselves. It may take some believing, but it's true.

Give each member of the group a pen and piece of paper. Ask them to think of situations or circumstances which have made them feel confused and/or afraid, or still do. You might like to start by sharing something that makes you feel uncomfortable.

When the group have completed writing on their pieces of paper, ask them to fold the paper into a small square and place it at the base of the candle which you have placed in the centre of the room.

**(Allow 5 minutes)**

Ask the group to be quiet as you light the candle. While everyone is quiet, read the following prayer:

Lord,
  at times –
  well, if I'm honest, quite a lot of the time –
  I feel as if my head
  is in a blender.
My thoughts whizz around,
  until everything
  is in a complete mess.
It makes my stomach churn,
  and my legs feel odd.
If I could close my eyes,
  stick my fingers in my ears
  and scream,
  then I would, if it made
  any difference
  to the way I feel.
You may have noticed
  that when I tried that last time
  people gave me funny looks
  and wondered
  if I was quite right in the head.
I couldn't admit to them
  that my head felt full of spaghetti
  and if I had told them
  it wouldn't have made any difference.
But telling you how I feel
  seems to make all the difference.
Thank goodness for that.

# Every shape, size, colour and hue

## Acts 11:1-18: Peter reports to the Church in Jerusalem

**Equipment:**
several tubes of Smarties (or similar coloured sweets)
dice
music and lyrics

Distribute the Smarties (or coloured sweets) randomly amongst the group. It doesn't matter if some of the group appear to have a few more sweets than others, it might add to the fun. Allocate a colour to each number of the dice, e.g. 1=red, 2=yellow and so on. There may be more than six colours but, again, that doesn't matter as long as you only allocate six numbers to six colours.

In turn, each member of the group rolls the dice and eats the sweet corresponding to the number they roll. If they haven't got the colour sweet that corresponds to the dice then they cannot eat any sweet. If a group member throws a 'six' on the dice, they can choose whether to eat the sweet relating to that number or try to swap one of their sweets with another group member for another colour. Continue rolling the dice in turn. Eventually, some of the group will have eaten all of their sweets, some will have colours which are not represented on the dice and some cannot roll the right number to finish eating their sweets.

**(Allow 10 minutes for this activity)**

It's surprising how quickly and easily we can become either prejudiced or intolerant. Take a look at 'As I come to you' by Mick Dalton (*World Wide Worship No. 1*) or 'Let there be love' by Dave Bilbrough (*The source,* 317).

**(Allow approximately 5 minutes)**

Ask the group how they felt during the sweet game.

- How quickly did they start to lose interest in certain coloured sweets?
- Did they try to 'swap' sweets for those that they favoured more?
- What point was the game trying to 'get across'?

**Read Acts 11:1-18**

Peter, once one of many fishermen to work along the shores of Lake Galilee, had come a long way since being called by Jesus to become a disciple. At first hand Peter had experienced the miracles and the heartache of Jesus' ministry. He'd followed, questioned and rejected Jesus but now had become a respected leader of the Christians in and around Jerusalem.

The message of Jesus had affected many people and many more were becoming followers of Jesus. The widespread 'Gospel' was attracting both Jews and non-Jews (Gentiles). This was beginning to cause a problem amongst those Jews who believed that the Gospel of Jesus was only for Jews. Peter had already been faced with this issue and was certain that God treated everyone the same (see Acts 10:34-36). Now the issue was becoming contentious, arguments and dissension threatened to cause a split within the Church.

Many of the people who had accepted God's message wanted the Gentiles to become just like them: Jews. This meant adopting the Jewish way of life and traditions, rejecting their identity and exchanging it for another. The bottom line was that the Jewish believers didn't feel they could accept the Gentiles for who they were.

Peter had to step in and relate what had happened in the town of Joppa, where God had insisted that prejudice and racial discrimination had no part in God's plans. Once the people heard what God had said and that the Holy Spirit made no distinction between Jew and Gentile, then the arguments stopped and everyone began to worship God.

Accepting people for what they are is never easy, particularly when someone behaves very differently from us. God looks on each one of us as equals. He loves us for who we are and not what we may become. If God accepts everyone, irrespective of history, tradition, behaviour or appearance, then perhaps we should do the same.

As a group, try to define the word 'prejudice'.

- Are we prejudiced at times without realising it?
- What about in sport?
- How do we feel when we see images of people suffering because of starvation, war, intolerance or hatred?
- Is anyone to blame for people being homeless?
- Are there other instances where prejudice is apparent?
- How do we react?
- Do we feel uncomfortable with people of another race, belief, tradition or lifestyle?
- How easy/difficult is it to see things from God's perspective?

**(Allow 5 minutes)**

Ask the group to be quiet for a few moments while you read the following:

Lord,
    I can appreciate the colours
    in a field full of flowers.
I can smell the richness
    of the differing scents
    as the breeze blows across every plant.
I can hear an orchestra
    of sounds in the air,
    with each whisper of life
    giving an identity,
    a unique expression
    of living
    in a world of variety.
I appreciate the difference
    in everything that surrounds me.
Each building, tree, flower or person
    combines to make
    a tapestry of existence.
Lord,
    thank you for being
    the creator of all things,
    the giver of life
    and a Father to humanity
    in a world of variety.